1

Still Standing

By: Tamika Zigler Dillard

www.createspace.com/7014292

www.amazon.com

First and foremost, I have to thank God for allowing me to write this book. I would also like to thank some very important people for always believing in me. My beautiful Mother Collisa Stanley, my husband Cory, my brothers Damon and Tyrone, and my three children, Jaquantis, Josiah and JaCory. They have always believed in me and that gave me the motivation that I needed to begin this writing journey, along with my beautiful cousin/baby sis Jerica that I love with everything in me. To my sister Latoya, our dad Ronnie made us sisters but our hearts made us friends, I love you beautiful.

I've been working on this book for quite some time now & the road was definitely not easy. It shouldn't have taken this long to write this book but life happens and road blocks are sometimes necessary for growth.

I had started writing quite a few books and the titles were going to be, "When the abused becomes the abuser" & "Hurt people hurt people", but God said no. He let me know that it is only by his grace that I am still standing. I am certainly not writing books to get rich. I just pray that my story will inspire others as they are on this journey called life and that God will get the glory out of all of our lives.

Contrary to how some others may believe, I whole heartedly believe that our God is Awesome, he always makes a way out of no way. What I love mostly about him is that even when we mess up, he loves us enough to not write us off.

Some people will say that they love you and that they have your back per say, but as soon as you need them, you will learn that they were never your real friends, just secret admirers or snakes in the grass awaiting your downfall. Please keep in mind that no matter how much a person may change their outward appearance with cosmetic surgeries, makeup, hair weaves, etc., if their intentions aren't good, their hearts are waxed cold.

Matthew 24:12 KJV- And because iniquity shall abound, the love of many shall wax cold.

The New International Version reads as thus: Because of the increase of wickedness, the love of most will grow cold. We are definitely living in those times, and the wicked are getting bolder as the days go by but in this season, God is about to reveal the wicked and put an end to all of this foolishness, so get right church and lets go home.

Just to take you into my world for a moment, I must share with you what made me the person that I am today.

As I was growing up, I use to watch men physically and mentally abuse my precious Mother, but she would still forgive them and wish them the best in life. I use to be angry because I didn't understand how she could be nice to these people, some of them being our relatives.

I wanted them to pay for hurting her but she would say, "Vengeance is mine saith the Lord". I wanted for vengeance to be mine! I now understand what she meant though, now it all makes sense.

Matthew 5:44 KJV- But I say unto you, Love your enemies, bless them that curse you, do good to them that hate you, and pray for them which despitefully use and persecute you.

I've learned throughout my upbringing to always forgive and to never judge because we never know what people are going through that makes them act a certain way. It is best to just pray for them and make peace if possible. Trust and believe that the same ones that you hurt when you are up, you will see them again & you may need them when you come back down so be careful not to burn bridges because there's no way to cross back over once it's burnt and destroyed. And again, be very careful when judging others because you know that if the tables were to turn, you would hate to be judged.

Matthew 7:1-5 KJV- Judge not, that ye be not judged. For with what judgment ye judge, ye shall be judged: and with what measure ye mete, it shall be measured to you again.

Truth be told, we have all made unhealthy or unwise decisions throughout life, therefore we really don't have a right to condemn another human being.

John 8:8 KJV- He that is without sin among you, let him cast the first stone.

We all know that there would be no stones being cast because we are all sinners saved by grace. Every saint has a past, and every sinner has a future so stop turning your nose up at others before your skeletons fall out. We all have a chapter in our book that we hope that no one will ever read.

Romans 3:23 KJV- For ALL have sinned, and come short of the glory of God.

I am a messenger from God, and I'm beyond grateful that he saved a wretch like me. I feel like I have to get this message out there because the things that I've been through in my life, the next person may not be able to handle if they don't know who to go to. I couldn't win these battles on my own; it took God to see me through.

DON'T JUDGE A BOOK BY ITS COVER

Many people look at me and they see a happy woman but they don't see my scars from the attempted suicides, neither can they see my tears from flashbacks late at night. My molestation didn't kill me, the strangulations and the physical abuse didn't take me out. That blow to my head affects my memory at times but I'm just grateful to be alive and functioning to the best of my ability. I'm definitely a survivor with the help of God and those closest to me and for that reason alone, I'm still standing.

GRATEFUL

I must say that I am beyond grateful to be alive. Satan has had it out for me since birth but I survived and I am still standing. My sweet Mother was told that she could never carry a child but by the grace of God she carried three of us. My father was not around due to the lifestyle that he chose to live which landed him in prison quite a few times. Not having him in my life was a big strike against me when it came to certain things. I was molested by a family member at the age of seven, and by my Mom's boyfriend, and other family members for many years, but I didn't share this information with her until I was giving birth to my first child.

His father and I went through things as most couples do and I was in tears during labor. My Mother asked me what was wrong and I broke down and told her everything. She got in the hospital bed with me, dried my tears and rubbed my back to try to calm me down. My Mom has always been my best friend and we have gotten even closer over the years. However, I looked for love and acceptance from these men and because my father wasn't around, I looked up to them. I would sit in their laps innocently but they took it the wrong way as if I wanted the attention and treatment that I was receiving from them but that was far from the truth. I just wanted to be loved, I wanted my dad but he was nowhere to be found. I wanted to be protected, instead I felt unloved and neglected. I would never release the names of these individuals in a book or online, and only those closest to me knows their identities, but if one of them happens to read my book, please know that I forgive you, not for you but for me. I choose not to hold on to it any longer because this is not my battle to fight, and vengeance is mine saith the Lord. Yes you scarred me, and you confused me, along with betraying me and my Mom's trust but we forgive you for our inner peace. I am free, praise the Lord I'm free, no longer bound, no more chains holding me. Now I know the true meaning of that song.

I was still looking for love and acceptance from a man as a teenager to replace my father. I got involved with several men who meant me no good. I was mentally, physically and emotionally abused by a few of these men but I would stay with them thinking that it was love. My Mom had boyfriends that would black her eyes, beat her badly and put guns to her head and she would stay with them, sometimes out of fear so I thought that staying wasn't so bad.

She wanted a father figure for my brothers and myself, but she chose the wrong men unfortunately as most of us do.

SIXTEEN AND PREGNANT

I got pregnant with my first child at the age of sixteen. I was scared to death and I didn't know how I was going to tell my Mother because she did not play. One day I wrote her a letter and slid it under her bedroom door. I explained to her how I "accidentally" got pregnant and I could hear her crying through the door. She felt so bad because she wanted so much more for me. I felt like a disgrace for disappointing her. My Mother told me that I was going to give birth to my baby and that she would help me with raising him so that I could finish high school and get me a job and she did just that. The sad thing is that I went through so much stress during my pregnancy until one day I just decided that I couldn't take being hurt anymore. That was the first time that I attempted suicide with a knife to my wrist. God sent my Mom into my room right on time and she took the knife from me and held me as I cried on her shoulders. She told me how beautiful and special I was and she promised to be there for me every step of the way and she definitely kept her promise. I went to high school during the day and worked at Hardees in the evening. I graduated a year late and although times were hard for me, I never gave up and I'm proud to say that I'm still standing. I survived in order to reassure you that there's nothing too hard for God!

LIFE'S JOURNEY

My life hasn't been easy by far. I've had two other children over the years and I was close to having a failed marriage. Although I'm not proud of that, it was all necessary for my growth.

My three children are my world and I wouldn't trade them for anything. They definitely hold me together when I'm falling apart. To this day, I keep pictures of my three boys in my car and on those days that I've felt like throwing in the towel, running my car off a cliff or contemplating a head on collision, I look at their pictures and smile. It's like I can hear them saying, "Keep going Mommy, we love you and need you" and that's all of the push that I need. The devil would like for me to believe that I'm worthless due to the mistakes that I've made in my past, along with my recent separation from my husband that lasted for nine months before we reconciled, but I refuse to believe that anymore. A pregnancy usually last for nine months, therefore I view this as my birthing process. Strength, patience and forgiveness were birthed from our pain. I had asked God for more patience and strength to make it from day to day but I had no idea as to why I would need it. I had to go through all of that in order to write this book, it just had to happen.

We all know that there can be no testimony without a test. How can I help someone else that may be going through the same thing unless I've been through it? Some of the things that I've been through in my thirty four years of living could've been avoided if it was up to me, but I've learned that everything happens by God's permission. Some things are blessings, while other things are lessons.

The devil had a plot but God had a plan. My life is not my own, I belong to God. This brings clarity to all of my many trials and tribulations that I survived. Look at me, I'm still standing.

BE ENCOURAGED, IT IS NOT OVER FOR YOU....

Not only did I have to go through those things to learn something myself, I went through those things to help you. I need you to keep on standing, I need you to survive. You have to know that you are not what happened to you. You are beautiful, you are special; you are more than a conqueror. Don't allow anyone to discourage you. They don't know that God chose you for a time such as this; therefore they will never understand your purpose. So what if they don't like you because you're peculiar and they don't understand you. What's understood by God don't need to be explained to man. In addition to that, they don't have to do either of the above, but they do have to love you in order to make it into heaven. Another thing to add to that; you can't pay any of your bills with their opinions so be encouraged my friend, it is not over for you.

PICKED OUT TO BE PICKED ON

Throughout my life it seemed as if I was picked out to be picked on. I never did fit in with the crowd.

I never thought that I was better than anyone else, I was just brought up with certain morals; therefore I chose not to hang out with certain type of people. On top of that, my Mom and my brothers were very strict and overprotective because I'm the baby (smile). This caused me to not have many friends and I was lonely at times but I was doing what was best for me. Don't get me wrong now, I've made my share of mistakes; sex before marriage, trying marijuana at the age of sixteen, lying and cheating to name a few so I'm not exempt from any of that. I'm human so that means that I am far from perfect. Another thing; I hated elementary school because I was bullied by other children and picked on because my Mom couldn't afford high priced name brand clothes and shoes like others could. I loved my Reebok Classics but no one else did. However; my Mom did the very best that she could and her best will forever be good enough for me. "They laugh at me because I'm different. I laugh at them because they are all the same." –Kurt Cobain

BLESSINGS AND LESSONS

We must understand that the plan for our lives was set before we were placed in our Mother's womb. Some of the things that we go through in life are lessons and if we don't pass the test we must retake it.

Life is definitely like a confused teacher, it gives you the test before the lesson. We will certainly learn to appreciate life's blessings once we see them for what they really are.

Some would argue that having children out of wedlock is a mistake, but I believe it to be a lesson that brought about a blessing, because no matter what goes on between the parents, a precious child was created, and no one can change that.

LIFE HAPPENS

I use to go throughout life being upset with myself if things didn't quite go as planned, until I realized that I can't control anyone but myself and that alone can be a task in itself (smile). So now when my car won't crank, or I happen to get a flat tire, and/or I have no money in the bank to fix these problems, I sit back and smile because things could always be worse. We often complain about bills while there's a less fortunate man/woman out there that wish they had a place to call home and some bills to pay. While we sit around and complain about our jobs, someone else is praying for a job. While we are sitting around complaining about our mates, someone is praying daily for a mate. While we are complaining about our children or our parents getting on our nerves, someone just received a phone call about their child or parent dying. We must understand that life happens and not everything can be prevented. Some stumbling blocks were placed in front of us to test our faith and to help us to grow. We must learn to appreciate each breath that God gives us and be grateful for the people that he has placed into our lives, because in the blink of an eye, it could all be gone.

BE GRATEFUL FOR WHAT YOU HAVE, BEFORE IT BECOMES A MEMORY OF WHAT YOU HAD…

IF TOMORROW NEVER COMES

What if this is it? What if tomorrow never comes? Are you satisfied with where you are in life? Did you reach some or all of your goals?

Did you forgive someone of their faults and ask for forgiveness for yours?

Did you always show love to your family members, friends and others? Did you pray enough?

Did you fast enough? Was that television show more important to you than helping that child with their homework?

Did you try hard enough to fight for that broken marriage or was that social media site more important?

What will people remember about you? Will you leave a great legacy behind, seeds of discord or financial burdens?

Did you give life your best shot? Will you be on your death bed with regrets?

Please do me a favor, if you're not pleased with the answers to those questions, do what you can do to change your outlook on life. We only get one shot at this thing called life so don't be so hard on yourself. (YOLO).

Remember to laugh a lot, forgive yourself and others and let us try to enjoy this beautiful life that we were blessed with just in case tomorrow never comes. Sometimes you find yourself in a tough situation, and sometimes in a tough situation, you find yourself. Don't just go through it, grow through it.

PAIN IS SOMETIMES NECESSARY FOR GROWTH...

NO LONGER BOUND

I am not my mistakes. I am not my disappointments. I am no longer in bondage. I have been forgiven and I have been set free. For many years I've walked around in shame because of poor deisions that I had made throughout life. I hated myself for silencing my pain. Again, my molestation started at the age of seven by a close family member and I hid it from my Mom out of fear of what she would do to them if she found out and because my molesters said that no one would believe me. Well one particular day, my Mom left my brothers and I with a family member while she walked up the road to Floyd's store to get us something to eat because it had been snowing and we didn't have much there. Well, this particular family member attempted once again to rape me but my oldest brother Damon woke up and caught him red handed. My brother hit him in the head with a beer bottle and he passed out in the floor. He was drunk and I was frightened because I just knew that he would get up and hurt my brother. My Mom came home in the nick of time and she was hurt when she found out what had happened. She screamed out "Why would you do this to my baby, I trusted you!" She checked my private areas to make sure I wasn't hurt; then she got me dressed and put him out of our apartment. She held me and said that she was sorry that this had happened; she then put me in the bed with her. After that had happened to me, I started wetting the bed until I was in middle school because I was scared to go into the bathroom. I thought that the monsters would get me. I couldn't go to sleepovers or anything because of my condition and the one time that I did go, I wet the bed and when this person told others about my accident, I was picked on in school for quite some time for something that I couldn't control, and that scarred me big time. The monsters created this problem for me. My molesters were the monsters that I was afraid of but I forgave them a long time ago, therefore I am no longer bound.

BROKEN PIECES

When you look at me, what do you see? Do you see a happy girl or just who I appear to be? Can you see the pain in my eyes, dark clouds or blue skies? Life has broken me down before, instead of living, I fantasized of dying more.

You seem confused but you shouldn't be, life had almost gotten the best of me. The more that I ran from demons, the more they chased after me. The more I said no, the more they'd say stop fighting it and just let it be.I've been to hell and back and I shall not return; I flunked the test the first time; there was a lesson to be learned.

You said that you see my beauty on the outside, but you overlooked the wrist cuts that I tried to hide. I've been broken into pieces a time or two, but grace and mercy pulled me through.

BETRAYAL

What you must understand is that betrayal usually comes from those closest to our heart and the pain that comes along with it can sometimes take years and years to heal, if it ever really does. It's like a bullet to the head but you survive and the memories are very much alive. It may have been days, weeks, months or years but the memories and thoughts never leave.

We often think that something is wrong with us when we are left to endure such pain but that type of thinking is far from the truth. Something is wrong with that person, not you. Most people struggle to like themselves so how can they love you?

I went through a situation in my teenage years that broke me down for sure. I was in love with a young man and I was sure to do everything right to make our relationship last only to be left feeling like something was wrong with me. When someone cheats on you multiple times and babies are born, that's something that could never be undone & if it's unbearable, do yourself a favor and move on.

I was pregnant too but stress caused me to lose my baby and that was a hard pill to swallow. I wrote a poem from my baby girl, it's like I could hear her talking to me. Lord knows I needed that closure.

HELLO MOMMY

Hello Mommy I love you so, you protected me by letting me go. I love it here and I love you too, Guess what Mommy? I look just like you. I hear that the earth is a scary place, but Mommy I'll always protect you like I did on yesterday. I looked down there and saw my brothers, they are really cool, please tell them to be good and to do good in school.

Oh Mommy, I met an angel here, and her name is Doreen, she looks out for me and shows me things.

I wish that you could meet her too, well I guess I'm late, she already knows you. Well Mommy it's time for our angel prayer, I'll whisper one for you. Please tell daddy that I'm watching over him too. Be good!

Rest in peace baby girl Rayeonna & my Auntie Doreen. Gone too soon but you all will never be forgotten. Stay strong Ma, GrannyMary, baby cuz/sis Jerica, Danielle, Joshua, and family.

<u>REST ON BABY GIRL</u>

Rest on baby girl; I guess that you were just too precious for this world. Although I never had the chance to hold you in my arms, I know that I would've kept you safe from harm. Why did you stop breathing on me? Did the stress of me crying make your little heart weak? I think about you all of the time, and picture you smiling at me in the sky. We will definitely meet someday, but until then watch over your family little Miss Raye Raye. I guess you died so that we could survive; what an angel you are, I'll always keep you in my heart, that way you'll never be far.

<u>WHERE IS THE LOVE</u>

I turned on the news and what did I see? Another person killed that looks like me. Another child lost his father, another Mother lost her son, All we are saying is "Stop killing us for fun!" Black Lives Matter, man to who? A dog's life is more important than me and you. I see your tears, I even smell innocent blood; please tell me where is the love? No it wasn't my father or child but they could be next, Lord please show yourself and loose the hex. What a cold world we are living in, we all know this to be true, Lord please reveal yourself, the world needs you. Send us a sign through an angel or a dove because people got me questioning, where is the love?

WHY DO I FEEL SO ALONE

Why do I feel so alone when God is on the throne, so many thoughts barricading my mind as if I'm running out of time. Lord, can you hear me, I'm crying out to you. Show yourself; please tell me what to do.

NOT FORSAKEN

I am more than grateful that God has never forsaken me even while I was in my mess. I am thankful that he didn't cut me off, although I deserved it. Grace and mercy surely did cover me and if it had not been for the Lord who was on my side, I never would've made it.

I tell you what my dear readers, Satan is real and all it takes is for you to let him get in your ear. Once he has the mind, the body will follow so please guard your ears.

POWER

I am sitting in my bedroom right now reflecting on a message that Pastor Bridgette Battles preached recently. I met her many years ago through my brother Damon and she has always been down to earth. She has been through her share of pain but she never lost her faith, and she is definitely one of my role models. Pastor Battles said that we have the power, but we must first identify who we are, define who we are, then work and execute the power and plan at the same time.

She explained how Peter walked on water by faith, but as soon as he took his eyes off of God, he began to sink. We must be very careful to not take our eyes off of the prize. I don't know about you but I don't want to sink, lose my way, and make hell my home. I've come too far, I've overcame so much, and I have too much to lose, therefore I can't turn back. My bible tells me that I have power and I believe it.

Mark 16:18 KJV- They shall take up serpents; and if they drink any deadly thing, it shall not hurt them; they shall lay hands on the sick, and theyshallrecover.
I HAVE THE POWER!!

WHAT'S GOING ON

We are living in a time where people will kill you and they could careless about the pain that your family will have to endure when they receive that phone call. I agree that BLACK LIVES MATTER; and I also agree that ALL LIVES MATTER, whether you are White, Black, Mexican, Chinese, Asian, Puerto Rican, Christian, Muslim, Jehovah witness, Jewish, etc. God created us in his image and he believed that we were to die for so he sacrificed his life so that we all would have a right to the tree of life. I refuse to live my life in fear because I know that although someone may be able to destroy the outward man, they could never destroy my soul.

Isaiah 41:10- Fear thou not; for I am with thee: be not dismayed; for I am thy God: I will strengthen thee; yea, I will help thee; yea, I will uphold thee with the right hand of my righteousness.

LOVE YOURSELF

Trust and believe that there will be days when you will feel like giving up, but I promise you that if you will just hold on, stand strong, and love yourself, you will be able to survive anything that may come your way. We know that trials only come to make us strong so don't lose sight of who you are, and keep striving to reach all of your goals. Go hard until your dreams manifest and your good becomes your best. Please keep in mind that self preservation is the first law of nature. It doesn't matter what others may think about you, what matters is what you think about yourself. We don't have to be a product of our past. Aren't you tired of only existing?

I know that I am, it is now my time to LIVE!

2 Corinthians 5:17- Therefore, if any man be in Christ, he is a new creature: old things are passed away; behold; all things are become new.

FAITH WORKS

Regardless of what you may have gone through, you can now look back and see that you made it. You survived the stormy weather. You kept the faith, and you finished the course like a good soldier.

That storm didn't get the best of you; you got the best of it because you remembered that faith works.

NO LIMITS

You must learn to not put limits on God or yourself. Stop limiting your ideas, dreams and goals. You can do all things through Christ, but the first step is to believe it and to know that you are more than a conqueror.

You don't have to live a mediocre lifestyle or even paycheck to paycheck. Go ahead and write that book (I did), start that business, or whatever it is that your heart desires. Make it happen for yourself and watch God take you further than you've ever imagined. He is a limitless God, there's no limit to what God can do, what he did for others, he can do the same for you.

Ephesians 3:20 NKJV- Now to him who is able to do exceedingly, abundantly above all that we can ask or think, according to the power that works in us.

YOUR PAST DOESN'T DEFINE YOU

As humans, we all have experienced set backs, disappointments, and pain. Some of us have experienced horrendous things, such as molestation, rape, mental and physical abuse and so forth but that doesn't have to define who we are. We have all even committed murder when we open our mouths to put another human down; yes we have killed them with our mouths.

Some look at murder by a weapon as the worst sin there is, but there's no big sin or little sin. Sin is sin and we will all be judged accordingly so please tread lightly in that area.

THE WEAPONS MAY FORM, BUT THEY SHALL NOT PROSPER

A lot of us will question God when things aren't going quite as planned in our lives, but this particular bible verse lets us know that no weapon that is formed against us shall prosper. We sometimes have to endure much in our walks of life but if we will endure until the end, we shall receive a crown. My eldest brother Damon was diagnosed with cancer some years back & at one time, things had gotten pretty bad. The doctor's had called the family in, and we traveled to Philadelphia PA from Martinsville VA to touch and agree that IT WON'T WORK! A few days after praying & singing in that hospital room, my brother rose up out of that bed praising God, singing, and speaking in tongues & we walked to the car singing "Never would've made it"! Evidently, they did not know the God that we serve.

We have lost a lot of family members due to that demonic force known as cancer but we refuse to go down without a fight. IT WON'T WORK!

Isaiah 40:31 KJV- But they that wait upon the Lord shall renew their strength; they shall mount up with wings as eagles; they shall run, and not be weary; they shall walk, and not faint.

Look at your neighbor and say, "It's in the word" (smile)

We have to believe what the word tells us because God promised us that his word will never return void. He loves us so much that he will reach way down into a pit to pick us up when we fall.

STOP PROSTITUTING GOD

At some point in our lives, we have all been guilty of treating God like a pimp or a prostitute. We call on him when we need him, then when he blesses us spiritually, financially, or physically, we let him go as if we don't need him anymore. As soon as all hell breaks lose and we need another fix, we call on him again. We must be very careful because we don't want to be in the hands of an angry God. We must also keep in mind that God don't need us, we need him!

Hebrews 10:31 KJV- It is a fearful thing to fall into the hands of the living God.

Don't give up on God because he won't give up on you, he is able...

FORGIVENESS HEALS

Stop dwelling on what they did to you & start being more concerned about what will happen to you, and your soul if you continue to hold on to that bad seed. Forgiveness is for you so let it go, and watch how you will start to blossom. We have all gone through something. Let go and let God. Live through it and survive.

HURT PEOPLE, HURT PEOPLE

This is so true, hurt people do hurt people. Have you ever been lied to, cheated on, lied on, abused, bullied, or talked about? I'm sure that you've answered yes to some or all of those questions. Well have you ever done any of those things to someone else? And if so, why did you? Is it because someone did it to you first? Did it make you feel better?

You probably said no to those questions. Why is that you think? It is because when we hurt others for what someone else did to us; that does nothing to better the situation. Just like you didn't deserve to be hurt; neither did they.

The abused became the abuser, and only God can fix your heart at that point.

THE FATHERLESS CHILD

Growing up, I was a fatherless child and that was some serious pain. I often questioned myself as to why my father didn't love me. I use to ask my Mom why he never came around. I often wondered why he wasn't around to protect me. My Mom would never talk badly about my dad but later on, I found out that he was in and out of prison, therefore he couldn't be around me. I hated myself, and I accepted less than I deserved in relationships because I did not know my worth. I thought that my father didn't love me and that made me abuse my self, as if that makes any kind of sense but I was young and hurting. I use to cut up my arms, legs and face just to feel the pain on the outside that I was feeling on the inside so that someone could understand my pain. I've suffered from low self esteem most of my life because of things that I went through but God showed me a beautiful woman in the mirror not to long ago, and you can't tell me that I wasn't beautifully and wonderfully made because I now know my worth. I now watch as my own child go through similar things and he often lashes out at me like I did to my Mom and others, but I now recognize that the anger that he has for the absent parent is sometimes reflected in how he treats others. No child was asked to be brought into this world, and what I can't seem to understand is how others will put their selfish wants before their child's needs. It is beyond me, but as long as I'm alive, my children will never want for anything. My father and I have gotten closer over the years, to God be the glory. Although he was hardly around when I was younger, I love him as if he was. Shout out to my dad, the one and only Ronnie Benton (smile). I didn't get his last name at birth because he wasn't around, and my Mom wasn't married to him.

My step father loved me and treated me as if I was his very own, and I love Mr. Steve Zigler for that. I will always have the upmost respect for him.

WEEPING MAY ENDURE FOR A NIGHT

As I was going through certain things in my life, I would recall this particular scripture in the bible. I love how it says "But joy cometh in the morning". Sometimes it seemed as though my night lasted forever. I yearned for my morning to come, but I've learned that God's morning and my morning are two different things. Everything that I've been through, I had to go through it in order to have a testimony. I am now reaping the benefits of those long nights, to God be the glory.

MAMA'S GIRL

Those that know me know that I am a true mama's girl. She is my best friend and she could never be replaced. She has earned that title for sure. I trust her more than anyone on this earth. Why, you may ask? Well it is because she loves me at my worst, she's always praying for me, and encouraging me, all while correcting me when I'm wrong. Another reason why is because when everyone else walked away, my sweet Mama stayed. She was my Mother and father growing up, and she worked hard to make sure we didn't go without. She showed Godly love to those that hurt her, and she showed me what forgiving and living was all about. She was my coach during labor with all three births of my children; she was at my high school graduation with my son, cheering me on when others doubted me. She was at my wedding; and she performed the wedding ceremony too. There's no one alive that could ever take her place. I'm definitely a mama's girl, and one day I'll give her the world.

LOVE CONQUERS ALL

Doesn't it feel good when you are loved? You give that same love away so freely because it was first given to you. Just as it is easy to curse someone out when you feel wronged, it is even easier to forgive them, love them from a distance, and pray that some day they will get it right. Keep in mind that your character isn't defined by how someone treats you, and it isn't justified by the lies that they told. It is simply determined by the way that you respond. My brother Damon always says that it's nice to be nice, and that is very true. My brother Tyrone always tells me that I need to think before reacting, and I've learned that thinking is very important, but sometimes I just don't feel like thinking (smile) and that has caused me a lot of pain. My brothers and I are very close and I am grateful for that. We can always depend on one another, and that makes life so much easier.

ONLY ONE WAY TO GO FROM HERE

Have you ever been so deep in a rut and you felt as if you couldn't get any lower? Well I've been there and it isn't a good feeling at all, but I've learned that when I am at my lowest point, that is the best time to pray. I'm already on my knees, and now I can work on getting back up because there's only one way to go from here and I plan to go up higher than I've ever been before.

Proverbs 24:16 KJV- For a just man falls seven times, and rises up again: but the wicked shall fall into mischief.

I CAN'T BREATHE

The worse feeling ever is not being able to breathe without assistance. The lack of love from loved ones can lead to depression and that is not a good feeling at all. I remember being in relationships but feeling as though I was single. At those moments I felt like I couldn't breathe due to the mistreatment. I'd have panic attacks and I would just have to leave out of the house to get some air. I've also had to visit a psychiatrist because I felt like I was dying or losing my mind at certain points in my life. Some things that I've experienced in my life with family and so called friends has distanced me more than you could ever imagine, but I had to do that in order to save myself from more heartache and pain. I've definitely learned that it is best to remove myself from situations such as these because no good thing will come from foolishness. I use to watch my Mom suffer from panic attacks, and she would go minutes without breathing. She is now healed, thanks be to God from whom all blessings flow, but she had to first learn how to distant herself in order to save herself. If it hisses like a snake, and it looks like a snake, guess what it is? I'm sure that you're intelligent enough to answer that question.(smile)

Like Maya Angelou said, "When they show you who they are the first time, believe them."

SPIRITUAL DEATH

There is nothing worse than being spiritually dead. It is a good thing to know bible verses, but it's even better to know how to fast and pray when you are going through certain test and trials. We also have to live a life that is acceptable to God in order for those prayers to be answered. If not, you will feel as if God doesn't hear you. Just know that you are not waiting on God, he is waiting on you.

BACK TO WHERE I BELONG

What a great feeling it is when you find out where you belong. It could mean being in the arms of your soul mate, or even living in an area that you love, but when you get back to that particular place, you will feel such calmness. It doesn't matter what may be going on around you, nothing will able to kill your vibe because this is where you belong. Many people have asked me why I decided to move from Martinsville VA to Greensboro NC seven years ago, and the answer is very simple. I lived here with my brother when I was a teenager. I loved it so much & I knew that this is where I wanted to be, so I made my way back to where I belong.

I want more for my children, and there are plenty of opportunities here for my family. We had a house built here, and we are here to stay.

Find out where you belong; then find your way back to that place of serenity.

HOME IS WHERE THE HEART IS

<u>WHAT ARE YOU WILLING TO SACRIFICE?</u>

Are you willing to sacrifice your sanity to keep that job or to keep someone happy? Are you willing to sacrifice your life for a friend? I am sure that you may have said no to those questions, but we have all been guilty of doing both of these things at some point in our lives. We love that nice paycheck so we continue to go to that job daily, and work around energy sucking vampires, only to go home crying daily while begging God for a change to take place. The sad thing is that every time he shows us a plan of escape, we allow money to become the motive for what we are willing to accept. We continue working on that same stressful job until we just can't take it anymore. In addition to that, we sometimes sacrifice our lives for so called friends. We try to be everything to everyone, to the point of losing ourselves. I'm sorry but I refuse to lose sight of my dreams and goals because it may upset a friend. I have spent many years trying to find myself, getting to know what makes me happy and so forth; therefore I refuse to sacrifice myself any longer. If you are my true friend, you will be happy for me, and if not, goodbye, I bid you God's speed. Dear readers: If they don't encourage you, inspire, or enhance you, then you must wish them well and let them go.

As my Bishop Sheldon McCarter has said many times before: In this season of my life, I can't afford to allow negative people into my circle.

LOSE THE NAYSAYERS OR LOSE YOURSELF IN THE PROCESS. CHOOSE WISELY!!

TOO BLESSED TO BE STRESSED OR TOO STRESSED TO BE BLESSED?

If you are going to proclaim to be a Christian or the righteous, we must choose blessings over stressing. I just recalled something that my Mom says often to me. If you are going to pray then don't worry, and if you are going to worry, then don't pray. I'm not saying that things won't get to you because they will. We are all human and subject to being stressed out from time to time but we must remember whom we serve. We have to trust that God will see us through no matter what we may encounter. I know without a doubt that I am too blessed to be stressed.

Ecclesiastes 9:11 KJV- I returned, and saw under the sun, that the race is not to the swift, nor the battle to the strong, neither yet bread to the wise, nor yet riches to men of understanding, nor yet favor to men of skill; but time and chance happens to them all.

Joshua 24:15 KJV- And if it seem evil unto you to serve the Lord, choose you this day whom ye will serve. As for me and my house, we will serve the Lord.

YOU SHALL LIVE AND NOT DIE, LIVE THROUGH IT

Do you ever feel as if God doesn't love you? You may have lost a loved one, a job, vehicle, or home? Do you sometimes feel as if God is punishing you because of that sickness that you have to endure? Dear readers, no matter what you may have to experience in this journey called life, be it cancer, lupus, multiple sclerosis, HIV, or any other sickness, you must know that it is all a part of God's plan for our lives. You never know who may be watching you as you fight to survive. You never know who may need that encouragement from you, so stop complaining, keep praying, keep fighting, and live through it.

LET GO AND LET GOD

I am sure that we have all heard that saying before. We must know that the battle is not ours, it is the Lord's. That battle that you have been fighting, stop giving it the energy that you have been giving it. It is not up to you to try and figure it out.

Stop dwelling on the negatives and start reflecting on the positives and allow God to be God. He promised to not put more on us than we can bear, but we keep picking those problems back up trying to handle it ourselves. Well it is now time for us to let go and let God have his way. You are not in this alone, there is someone bigger than you that will go to war on your behalf so please learn to give all of your problems to him and I promise you that you will not regret it. Furthermore, stop telling God about that mountain and start telling that mountain (Goliath) about your God!

1 Peter 5:7 KJV- Casting all of your cares upon him, for he cares for you.

I would now like to take the time out to thank you for supporting me by purchasing this book. I feel as though someone's life depended on this book being written and to be quite honest, writing has been my healing and escape from things that are happening around me. I didn't tell many people about this book that I was working on because I know that the devil listens too and I didn't need any blessing blockers slowing down my progress. I would also like to thank a few of my awesome friends that are very dear to my heart. Thank you Lynn, Dena, Ernessa, and my friend/neighbor Sharon for always making me feel special even on my down days.

Sharon and Ernessa, these ladies night out events have changed my life for the better because I was always a loner. I was shy and scared to get close to others out of fear of getting hurt, but you all have shown me nothing short of what true friendships and Godly love is all about. I love you all, and I thank God for each and every one of you.

Tamia Draper- You did an amazing job on my makeup for my photoshoot. Thank you again!

Bianca Davis- My hairstylist at Posh Millenium: Thanks so much!

Catherine Forbes Hairston-Photographer at Your Vision Photography: Thank you so much for taking these amazing pictures of me at a last minute notice.

Another thing to add: My coworkers use to wonder why I would always keep my notebook on me and the reason is because my thoughts never stop. A dear friend had advised me to take a notebook to work & write down my thoughts & that was the best advice ever. When I don't even be thinking about writing; words, poetry, and songs keeps popping up in my head.

I'm working on a few more things as well, but I wanted to publish this book before I start my last semester of college because time gets away from me very quickly, especially while I'm working full time, attending college online full time, being a full time Mother to three awesome children. One more thing before you go please. I would like to share some of my poetry writings with you. This book was written, edited, and self published by me with the help of God. If I never sale a book, I want you to know that I am very proud of myself. These poems will explain how I've felt recently and throughout life with the many things that I have faced. Thanks again for taking the time out of your busy schedule to read my book. It is by the grace of God that I am in my right mind and still standing.

STAY

I now understand why I must pray, I even understand why I pushed you away. I've learned to hate love and to love hate, when people get too close, I push them away. I promise that I forever want you to stay, thanks for loving me this way.

WHY

Why do I write, you ask, I write to be an inspiration. Why do I pour my heart out, I'm trying to save a nation. I have three mouths to feed; I have to save my babies. I have to give it all I got, can't feed them with maybe's. Maybe I'm right or maybe I'm wrong, I just don't want there name to be another hash tag in a song. They say that black is whack and white is right, I say love trumps hate, let's end the fight. So you ask again why do I write let's end this race war, it's time to unite.

LOVE AND PAIN

Love is pain; it's such a scary thing. Wait, Am I speaking of true love or infatuation? You build me up to break me down, man my heart needs a vacation. You just proved again that you're not too brilliant; I just proved again that I'm one in a million. Pain is inevitable, suffering is an option; you just threw me away like an illegal adoption.

I guess that this is the price that I'll have to pay, for openly giving my heart away, but I will no longer accept the rain, you're no longer my love and pain.

UNFAITHFUL

He use to ask me why am I so hateful, I use to ask him why is he so faithful. I thought he was weird for loving me so hard, why would he want me, I'm so broken and scarred.

While he was out working, another man was out lurking. Why he loves me so I don't know but I'm grateful, never will I again be so foolish and unfaithful.

KARMA

What is your name, who is your mama? Why do you taste just like karma? I taste every mistake and every decision, Karma I saw you coming, it was revealed in a vision. Okay now you can stop because this really hurts, I guess the grass was greener, it just needed work. Next time I will think before I react, and not be an accessory before or after the fact.

HURT PEOPLE

Hurt people do hurt people, I know this to be true, but if I could rewind time, I'd never hurt you. You have certainly made my life complete, and in your arms is where I want to be. First I want to lay on your chest and hear your heartbeat, next I want you to massage and tickle my feet. Then I'll let you into my soul, please hold me tight and never let go. They say that all people should be treated equal, so let's go and help these hurt people.

WORTHLESS

Why do I feel so worthless, Why am I still trying to find my purpose? This pen and paper is my way of escape, guess I hid it for years, just like that rape. The bullet missed me, man that was a blessing, I guess I'm worthy now, I just made a confession. Writing is my healing, releasing all pain, I'm tired of this feeling. Now I'm revealing and learning my purpose, no longer will I feel so stupid and worthless. If I must let you go, that's fine too, but I have to love me even without you. Marriage is sacred, they teach us that in Christianity, but this is some work, I'm just trying to keep my sanity.

REACH ONE

I've been tested, arrested & physically molested. I was headed to hell but God turned around and blessed it. A true survivor, that's who I am, neglected by loved ones that I call my fam. I survived what was meant to kill me, grace and mercy just wouldn't let it be. Raised by a single parent, black skin, dang two strikes already against me, all lives matter huh, well let's see. I refuse to stress over presidency, I answer to God only, but just please don't disrespect me. They say each one teach one, I wrote this book so that I could reach one. The first law of nature is self preservation, come on people, lets go and save a nation.

Please remember that we are victors, not victims, and that we are victorious. I pray that my book will inspire you to write the book that is inside of you. May God bless you.

No more following Satan, he's too demanding, my faith is the reason that I'm still standing!

Another thing that I must add to this ending is that if you are blessed to meet a genuinely good man or good woman, please hold on to them; spoil them & love him/her as if it's your last day on earth because it very well could be. May God bless us all.

VICTOR- A person who defeats an enemy or opponent in a battle, game, or other competition.

VICTIM- A person harmed, injured, or killed as a result of a crime, accident, or other event or action. A person that is tricked or duped; ex: the victim of a hoax.

VICTORIOUS- Having won a victory; triumphant.

Romans 8:37-39 KJV- Nay, in all these things we are more than conquerors through him that loved us. For I am persuaded, that neither death, nor life, nor angels, nor principalities, nor powers, nor things present, nor things to come. Nor height, nor depth, nor any other creature, shall be able to separate us from the love of God, which is in Christ Jesus our Lord.

Doreen and Doris:

You both were gone before we knew it, and only God knows why. You never said that our last hug & kiss would be our final goodbye. On earth I loved you both, in death I love you still, I swear that I still don't understand this, but it was in God's will. I promise you that the family will be okay, and I look forward to seeing you both on that sweet glorious day. Rest in peace my beautiful Aunties: Marilyn "Doreen" Stanley & Doris Zigler Pilson. You were both gone too soon but you will never be forgotten.

I've lost a lot of awesome family members throughout my lifetime but these two hit harder than any other. Doreen and I were very close. She was more like a second Mother than an aunt, and a day doesn't go by that I don't think about her. Although Doris was my Aunt by marriage (My Mom married her brother over 30 years ago), she always told me that I was her niece no matter what. I had just taken her out for breakfast less than two weeks before we lost her in a head on collision. I have to stop right now because I'm getting too emotional. REST EASY MY LOVES!! Save a spot for me.

ABOUT THE AUTHOR

TAMIKA Z. DILLARD IS A SURVIVOR BY THE GRACE OF GOD AND SHE FEELS AS THOUGH SHE WAS SENT BY GOD TO GIVE A MESSAGE. FROM BEING MOLESTED AS A CHILD AND SUICIDAL, TO OVERCOMING AND BEING A SURVIVOR. SHE BELIEVES THAT THERE IS A PURPOSE FOR HER LIFE. TAMIKA FEELS AS THOUGH SHE SURVIVED IN ORDER TO SHOW YOU HOW TO MENTALLY SURVIVE PAINFUL MEMORIES AND FLASHBACKS. SHE IS MARRIED TO CORY DILLARD & THEY ARE BLESSED PARENTS OF THREE AWESOME YOUNG MEN THAT THEY LOVE MORE THAN LIFE ITSELF. TAMIKA WORKS FULL TIME AS AN OPERATIONS REPRESENTATIVE IN LOGISTICS AT CH ROBINSON, AND SHE WORKS PRN AS A CNA MENTOR WITH WELLSPRING HOMECARE, WORKING ONE ON ONE WITH THE ELDERLY POPULATION. SHE IS ALSO A CURRENT STUDENT AT GUILFORD TECHNICAL COMMUNITY COLLEGE. TAMIKA LOVES SERVING OTHERS, THAT'S A TRAIT PASSED DOWN FROM HER MOTHER; THEREFORE HER CAREER FITS HER LIFESTYLE PERFECTLY. SHE ATTENDS GREATER CLEVELAND AVENUE CHRISTIAN CHURCH IN WINSTON SALEM, NC UNDER THE LEADERSHIP OF BISHOP SHELDON MCCARTER, AND SHE WROTE THIS BOOK WITH HOPES THAT HER TRANSPARENCY WILL SAVE A LIFE AND/OR A MARRIAGE.

Copyright © [2017]   Tamika Zigler Dillard
Independent Publisher

www.ingramcontent.com/pod-product-compliance
Lightning Source LLC
Chambersburg PA
CBHW060135050426

42448CB00010B/2131